Mundi's World

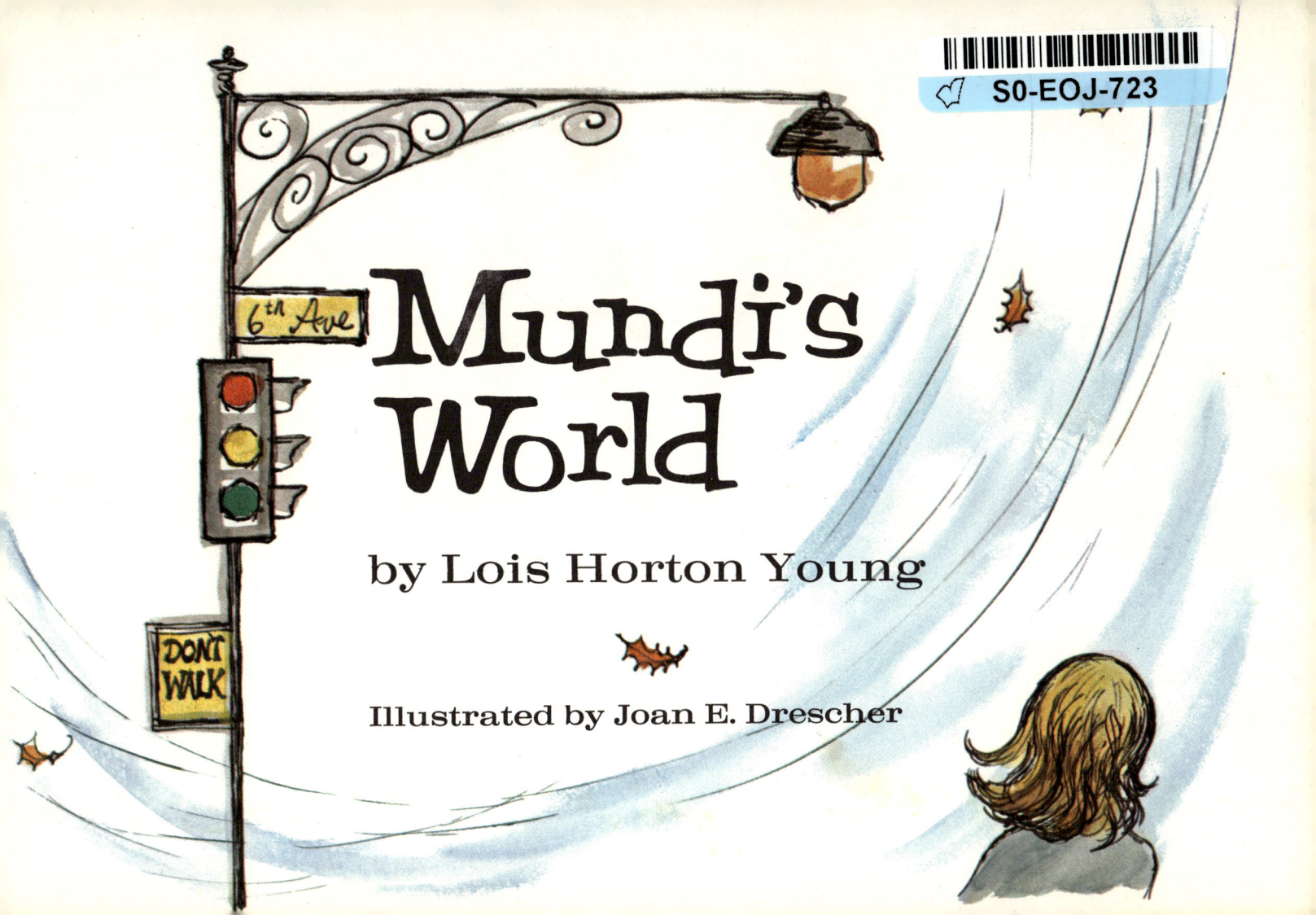

by Lois Horton Young

Illustrated by Joan E. Drescher

This book is part of the Encounter Series of the Church of the Brethren for use in the church school or other educational settings. The Encounter Series has been developed cooperatively with the American Baptist Convention, the Christian Church (Disciples of Christ), and the Church of God (Anderson, Indiana). Basic editorial decisions were made by an editorial team.

© H. W. Richardson 1970

Church of the Brethren General Offices
Elgin, Illinois

Printed in the United States of America

Mundi has a world to see and to know.
She has a world of things to use
and a world of people to love.

There is nighttime to enjoy —
a sky far and wide,
a shining moon 'way off in space,
stars that look like tiny twinks of
light.

Lights blink out over the city:
    blue-green lights at the expressway
        entrance,
    lights in the tall buildings,
    a light in Mundi's own apartment to shine
        till bedtime.

There is daytime with things to see and hear and feel.
A puppy is running down the street.
A tree is growing out of the pavement.
A pot of flowers is on the windowsill.

Mundi listens to horns and sirens in the street.
She feels wind touching her face and the sun is hot.

Mundi's brother comes out of the house.
"Come on, Mundi," Steve calls.
"We have to buy some onions."

At the market the stands are full of fruits and vegetables.
"Good morning!" smiles Mr. Julian. "What can I do for you?"
"We need a pound of onions," Steve tells him.
"One pound of onions coming up," says Mr. Julian. "Anything else?"
"That's all today," Steve says.

Mundi leans against the tree growing out
of the pavement and looks at her house.
It is a home with people in it who
love her.

Inside, there are things to laugh at and talk about.
There is someone to help her when she scratches her knee.
There is someone to knit a warm sweater for her.
When Mundi gets into bed, there will be someone to kiss her goodnight.

Mundi has friends to play with.
    Bang! Peter comes out of his door.
        "Hi, Mundi!" he calls.
    Bang! Carolita comes out of her door.
        "Hi, Mundi!" she calls.
    "Hi!" Mundi runs to meet them.
    "What shall we play?" she asks.

"We can play with my yo-yo," Peter offers.
"We can play with Romelo." Carolita holds out her little plastic donkey.
"We can play with my drumsticks," Mundi suggests.

Some days Peter's mother takes him to visit his Aunt Leah, and Carolita's grandmother takes her along when she goes to pay the gas bill.

"Good-bye!" Mundi watches them go. Mundi sits down on her front step. No one to play with! No one to share her two drumsticks with!

Along comes the postman.
"Good morning, Mundi!" he says. "No mail for you, but a letter for Mr. McGrew."
"I'll take it up to him," Mundi offers, and skippety-hops up the steps with Mr. McGrew's letter.

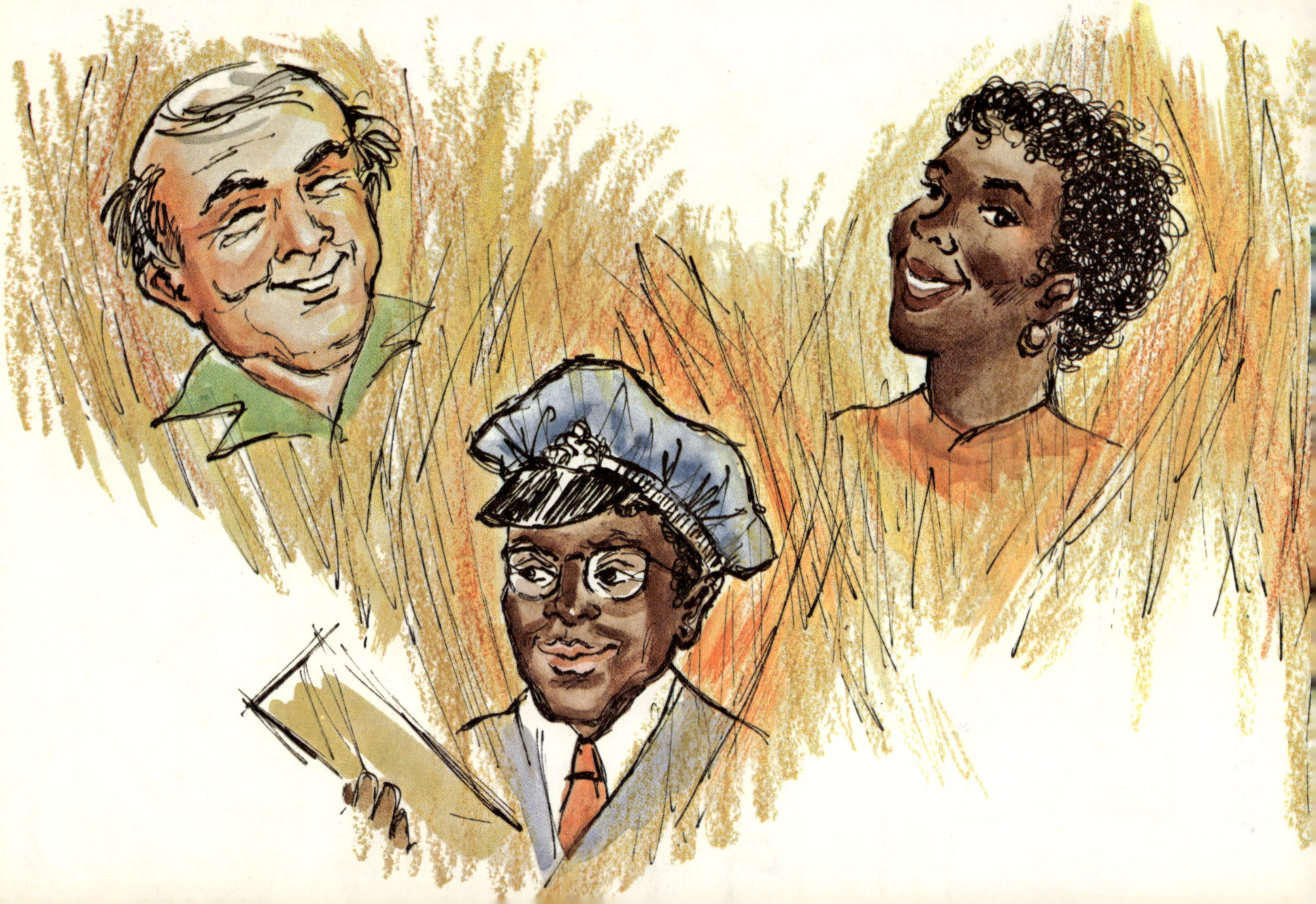

Mundi has a world of neighbors:
  Mr. McGrew, who lives upstairs;
  the postman, who brings the mail;
  Peter's mother, Mrs. Anders;
  Carolita's grandmother, Mrs. Gomez;
  and Mr. Julian at the market.
Mundi tries to count them and runs out
  of numbers.

When Mundi is thirsty she goes to the
sink and turns on the faucet.
"Bubble, bubble, swish!" The water runs
into her glass until it is full.

Push! She turns the faucet off. "Water is to use and not to waste," she remembers. "That's what Mr. McGrew says."

So Mundi's world is full of things to use —
things that are part of God's plan:
> The water in the faucet and down in
>   the harbor;
> the air, the sky;
> the tree, and flowers in a pot;
> the puppy;
> fruits and vegetables and nuts;
>> eyes for seeing,
>> and ears for hearing;
>> a mouth for tasting and talking,
>> and hands and feet to help.

And Mundi's world is full of other things —
things made by people who are part of God's plan:
> the markets, the lights, the expressway,
> the books, the yo-yo, the plastic donkey,
> the buildings in the city,
> a warm sweater, and the faucet.

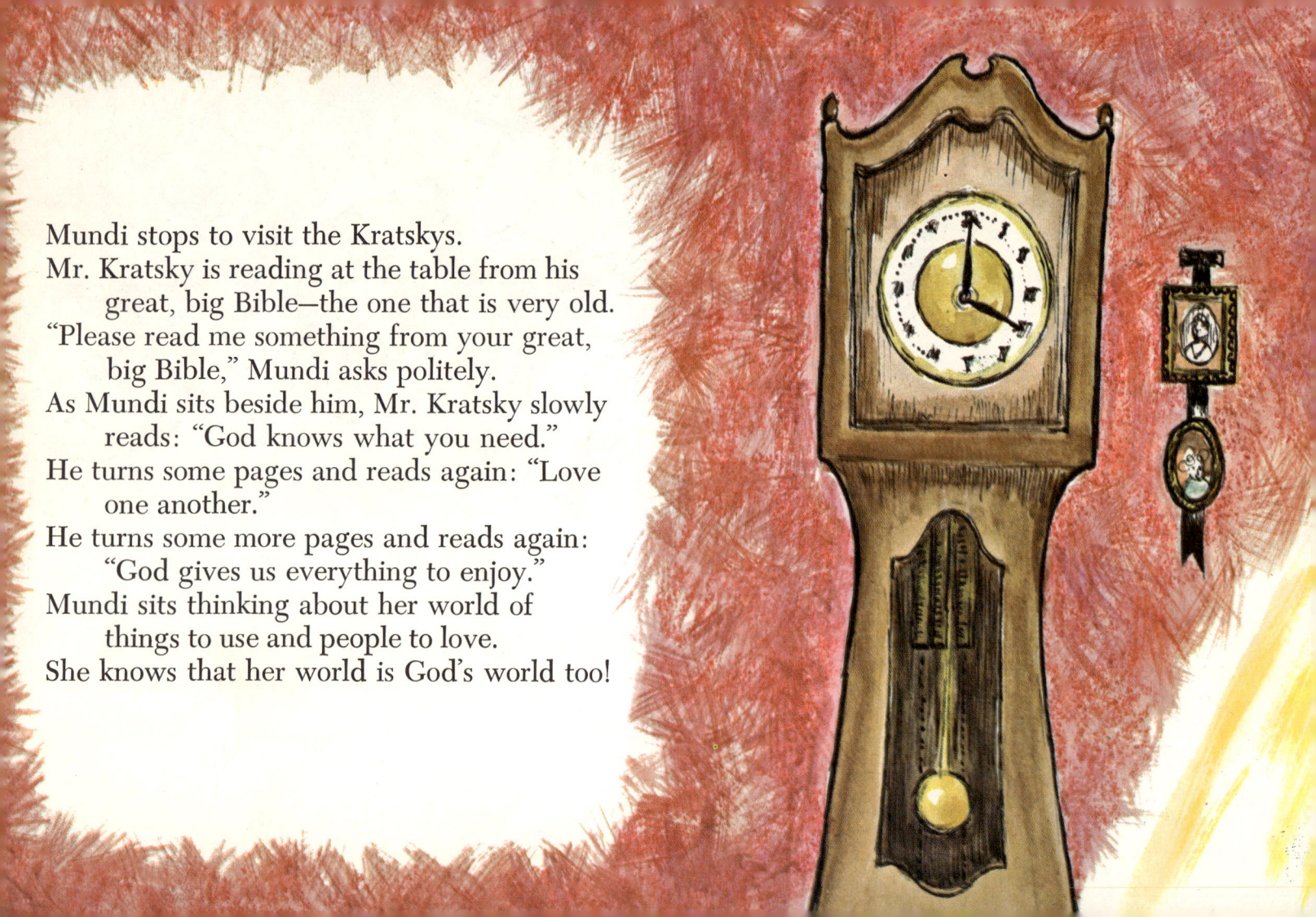

Mundi stops to visit the Kratskys.
Mr. Kratsky is reading at the table from his great, big Bible—the one that is very old.
"Please read me something from your great, big Bible," Mundi asks politely.
As Mundi sits beside him, Mr. Kratsky slowly reads: "God knows what you need."
He turns some pages and reads again: "Love one another."
He turns some more pages and reads again: "God gives us everything to enjoy."
Mundi sits thinking about her world of things to use and people to love.
She knows that her world is God's world too!

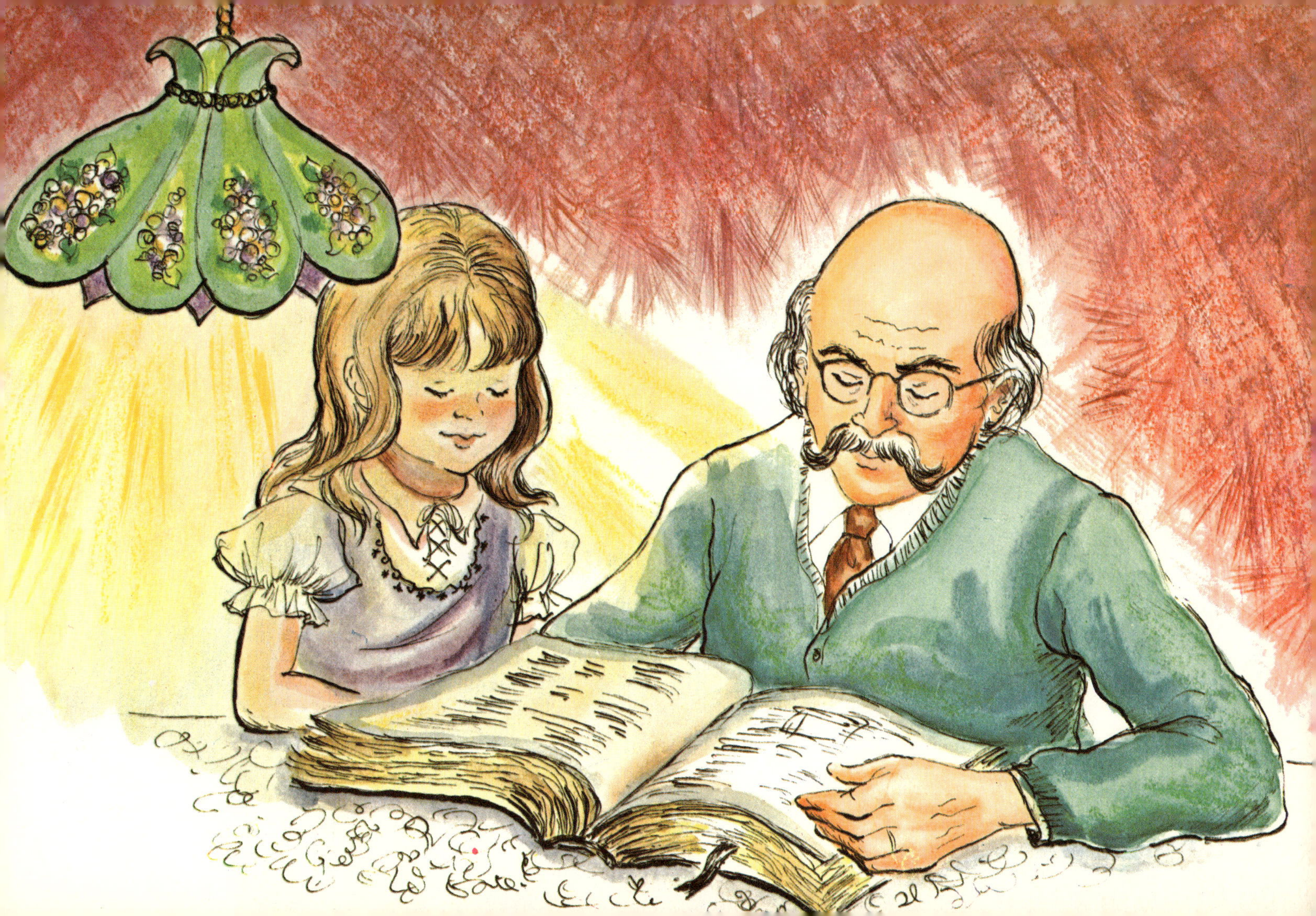

To the Adult Who Reads This Book to a Young Child:

A Child's World of Things and People

This book asks a child's questions:
    What is in my world?
    Where did my world come from?
    What is mine?
    What is yours?
    What is ours?
    What are things for?
    What are people for?

In the book Mundi begins to find some answers. She has eyes and ears to make her discoveries, and a mind for thinking things over; and there are people in her world who help her to understand.

We hope that the child who turns the pages of this book and listens while you read will ask some of the same questions, and be able to think in his own terms about his own world. We hope he will begin to find some of his own answers — answers that in him will stir wonder, certainty of God's loving-kindness, and his own need to respond gratefully and responsibly to God's love.